THE ULTIMATE NEW ZEALAND 2023 TRAVEL GUIDE

A PERFECT FIRST-TIME VISITOR GUIDANCE TO THE LAND OF THE LONG WHITE CLOUD (NEW ZEALAND)

D1104781

Mary Romero

TABLE OF CONTENTS

MAP OF NEW ZEALAND

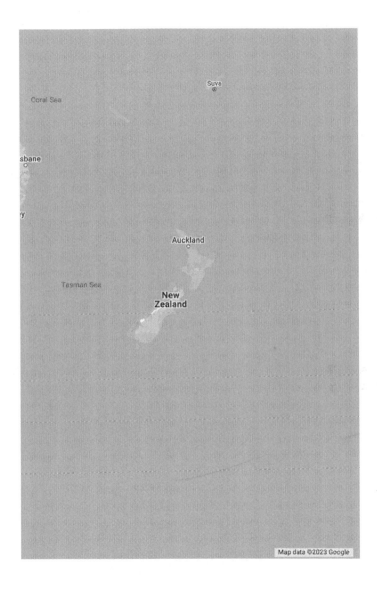

MAP OF AUCKLAND

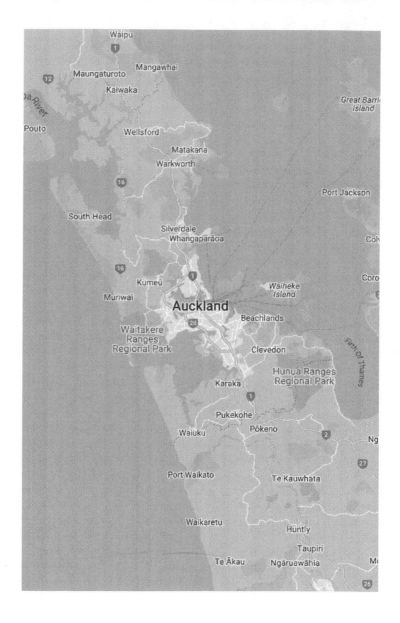

MAP OF CHRISTCHURH

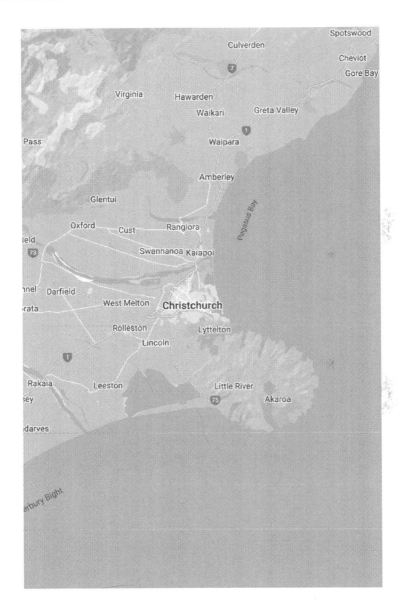

MAP OF QUEENSTOWN

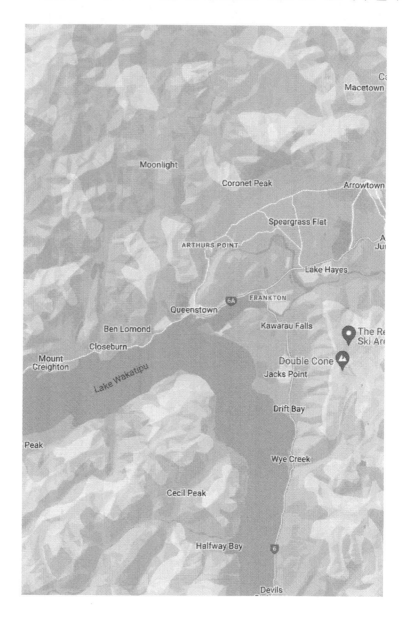

MAP OF HAMILTON

MAP OF TAURANGA

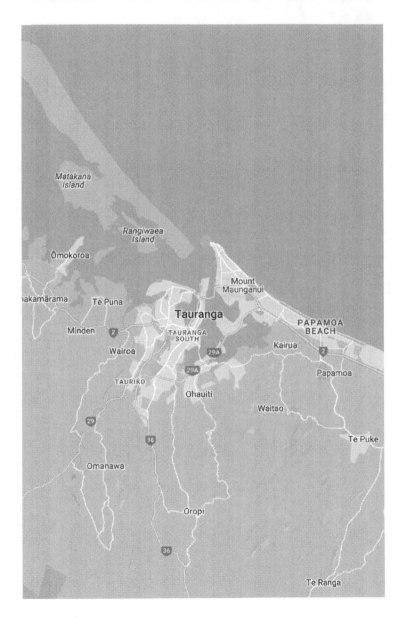

MAP OF DUNEDIN

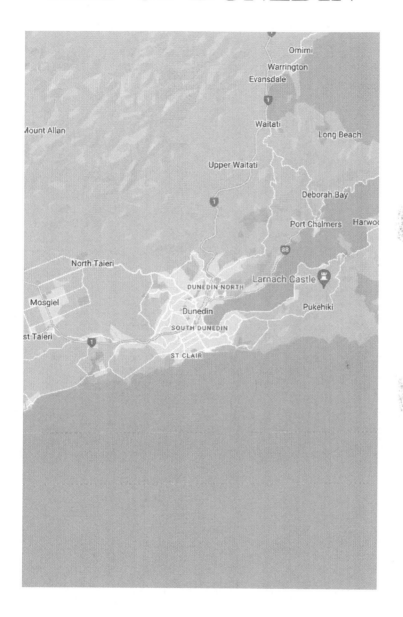

INTRODUCTION

Welcome to the ultimate guide to New Zealand in 2023! This guide is a comprehensive guide to exploring the stunning landscapes, vibrant culture, and unique wildlife of the Land of the Long White Cloud. From the beautiful beaches of the North Island to the rugged wilderness of the South Island, New Zealand has something for everyone. We'll delve into the country's rich history and culture, provide an overview of the best places to visit, and share tips for making the most of your New Zealand experience.

New Zealand is a country of contrasts. From the cosmopolitan cities of Auckland and Wellington to the small, rural towns of the South Island, New Zealand offers something for everyone. The landscape is diverse, ranging from lush green rolling hills and sandy beaches to rugged mountain ranges and ancient glaciers. While the country is geographically small, its culture is as diverse and dynamic as its landscape. Maori culture is deeply embedded in New Zealand's history, and its influence can be seen in the country's art, music, and food. In this guide, we'll explore the best places to visit in New Zealand in 2023.

We'll discuss the best activities and attractions in each region, as well as the best time of year to visit each region. We'll also look at the best places to stay and the best places to eat. We'll provide advice on how to get around the country, as well as tips for making the most of your New Zealand experience. New Zealand is home to a wide range of many outdoor activities. From hiking and mountain biking to kayaking and surfing, there's something for everyone. We'll discuss the best hiking trails in the country, as well as the best spots for biking and kayaking. We'll also provide information on the best places to surf, as well as the best places to go fishing. New Zealand is also home to a range of wildlife, ranging from the iconic kiwi to the majestic whale. We'll discuss the best places to see wildlife, as well as the best areas for birdwatching. We'll also provide information on the best places to go whale watching. New Zealand is also home to a range of unique and interesting cultural experiences.

We'll discuss the best places to learn about Maori culture, as well as the best places to experience the country's unique food, music, and art. We'll also provide information on the best places to learn about the country's unique flora and fauna. Finally, we'll provide tips for making the most of your New Zealand experience. We'll discuss the best ways to travel responsibly, as well as the best ways to experience the country's unique culture and wildlife. We'll also provide information on the best ways to stay safe and healthy during your travels. We hope that this book will be a valuable resource for anyone planning a trip to New Zealand. With the right planning and preparation, your experience of the Land of the Long White Cloud will be an unforgettable one. So get ready to explore the best of New Zealand in 2023! Happy exploring!

CHAPTER 1

ABOUT NEW ZEALAND

History

New Zealand is an island nation located in the southwestern Pacific Ocean, approximately 1,500 kilometers east of Australia. It is comprised of two main islands - the North Island and the South Island - as well as numerous smaller islands. It has a long and fascinating history which spans centuries and has been influenced by numerous cultures and peoples. In this lengthy write-up, we will explore the history of New Zealand, from its earliest inhabitants to the present day.

The earliest known inhabitants of New Zealand were the Māori, who arrived in the 13th century from their homeland of Hawaiki. They established numerous settlements throughout the islands and developed a rich culture and traditional lifestyle. The Māori were a hunter-gatherer people and were also skilled fishermen and farmers. They developed a complex social and political structure, which was based on their traditional belief system. The next major milestone in New Zealand's history was the arrival of Europeans in the late 18th century. The first Europeans to reach New Zealand were the crew of the British ship HMS Endeavour, who arrived in 1769.

This voyage was led by the famous explorer Captain James Cook. Cook mapped much of the coastline of the two main islands and also made contact with the Māori people. Following Cook's voyage, numerous other European ships arrived in New Zealand and the country began to be colonized by the British. In 1840, the Treaty of Waitangi was signed between the British and the

Māori chiefs. This treaty established the British colony of New Zealand and granted the Māori people certain rights and protections. However, the treaty was not always honored, and the Māori people suffered greatly over the following decades. The 19th century saw the arrival of many more European settlers, and the country began to rapidly develop. The British government continued to exert its influence over the colony, and the Māori people faced further discrimination and marginalization.

In 1893, New Zealand became the first country in the world to give women a chance to vote just like the men do. In the early 20th century, New Zealand fought in the First World War, and suffered a large amount of casualties. In the aftermath of the war, the country experienced a period of economic and social prosperity. This was followed by the Great Depression in the

1930s, which brought hardship and suffering to the people of New Zealand. In the 1940s and 1950s, New Zealand's economy began to recover and the country experienced a period of economic growth. From the late 1960s onwards, New Zealand began to develop its own identity and culture, and the Māori people experienced a period of cultural revival. This period also saw the development of the welfare state, and the introduction of a number of social reforms.

Today, New Zealand is an independent nation and a member of the Commonwealth of Nations. It has a diverse and vibrant culture, and is one of the most progressive and prosperous countries in the world. The Māori people have regained much of their traditional lands and have an important role in the country's culture and politics. New Zealand is also a popular tourist destination, known for its stunning natural beauty and unique culture. In conclusion, New Zealand has a long and fascinating history which spans centuries and has been influenced by numerous cultures and peoples. From its earliest inhabitants to the present day, the country has experienced a range of different events and developments which have shaped its identity and culture. Today, New Zealand is known for its stunning natural beauty and unique culture.

Culture

New Zealand is a beautiful nation, boasting picturesque landscapes, a rich and vibrant culture, and a strong sense of national identity. This small island nation, located in the South Pacific Ocean, is home to a multicultural population, a thriving economy, and a rich history. From its indigenous Māori heritage to its European settler presence, New Zealand's cultural landscape is diverse and multifaceted.

In this guide, we explore the culture of New Zealand, examining the various influences that have shaped this unique nation. The Māori are the indigenous people of New Zealand, and their culture has had a profound influence on the nation's current identity. The Māori first arrived on the islands of New Zealand around 800-1000 years ago, and their traditions and beliefs remain a major part of the country's cultural landscape.

Māori culture is based on a strong sense of family and community, as well as a deep reverence for the natural environment. Māori art, language, and music are highly valued and celebrated in New Zealand, and the traditional Māori greeting of 'Kia Ora' has become ubiquitous throughout the nation. European settlement in New Zealand began in the late 18th century. The first settlers were mainly British, and this influence is still evident in everything from the architecture of the country's cities to the language spoken by its people.

English is the official language of New Zealand, and most of the country's population speaks it as their first language. In addition, New Zealanders often use the words 'Kiwi' and 'Kiwiana' to refer to their national identity, drawing from the native kiwi bird. New Zealand is also home to many other ethnic groups, including Polynesian, Asian, and European immigrants. This diversity has created a unique cultural mashup, with different traditions and beliefs coming together to form the nation's unique identity. From the Māori haka to the vibrant music and art of the Polynesian population, the cultural landscape of New Zealand is a colorful mix of influences.

New Zealanders are known for their laid-back, relaxed attitude, and this is reflected in their culture. With its stunning landscapes, outdoor activities, and relaxed lifestyle, New Zealand is often seen as an idyllic place to live. Even the nation's capital of Wellington has been likened to a 'village in the city' due to its small-town feel. This relaxed attitude toward life is reflected in the country's culture, and it is also evident in the friendliness and hospitality of its people. The cultural landscape of New Zealand is unique and multifaceted, combining the influences of its indigenous Māori heritage with the many other ethnicities and traditions that have come to call the nation home. From its picturesque landscapes to its laid-back attitude, New Zealand is a truly special place, and its culture is something to be celebrated.

Geography

New Zealand is an island nation located in the South Pacific Ocean, southeast of Australia. It is composed of two main islands—the North Island and the South Island—as well as numerous smaller islands. It has a population of over 4.5 million people, the majority of whom are of European descent. The country is renowned for its stunning natural beauty, with majestic mountain ranges, lush forests, and dramatic coastlines.

The geography of New Zealand is varied and complex, with diverse landscapes that range from rugged alpine peaks to rolling hills and plains. The North Island is dominated by the central plateau, a large area of rolling hills and plains. This plateau is surrounded by mountains, the highest of which is Mount

Ruapehu, which reaches an altitude of 2,797 meters. The South Island is more mountainous, with many of the highest peaks located in the Southern Alps. The highest peak in the country is Mount Cook, which reaches an altitude of 3,724 meters. New Zealand is also home to numerous rivers, lakes, and wetlands.

The Waikato River is the longest in the country and drains much of the North Island. There are also many lakes throughout both islands, the largest of which is Lake Taupo. The country's many wetlands are important habitats for a variety of wildlife, and some of them are protected as national parks. New Zealand has a mild temperate climate, with warm summers and cool winters. The warmest months are December and January, while the coldest months are July and August. The country also experiences significant rainfall throughout the year, with the wettest months being February and March. New Zealand's geography also includes numerous islands. The two main islands are separated by the Cook Strait, and there are also many smaller islands scattered throughout the country. Some of these islands are inhabited, while others are uninhabited and serve as nature reserves.

The largest of the inhabited islands is the Chatham Islands, which is located off the east coast of the South Island. New Zealand's geography has played an important role in shaping the country's culture and history. The rugged alpine terrain of the South Island has helped to give the country its reputation for adventure activities, such as skiing and mountain biking. The islands of the South Pacific have also been an important part of the country's history, with the Maori people having a strong presence in the region. In conclusion, New

Zealand's geography plays a major role in its culture and history. The country's varied landscapes, from rugged peaks to rolling plains, provide a stunning backdrop for outdoor adventures and exploration. Its many rivers, lakes, and wetlands are also important habitats for a variety of wildlife. Finally, its islands in the South Pacific are a reminder of the country's rich cultural heritage.

CHAPTER 2

PLANNING YOUR TRIP

Budgeting

As a tourist or visitor to New Zealand, budgeting is an essential part of your trip planning. With its incredible landscape, unique culture, and varied activities, it can be easy to get carried away and overspend. However, with careful planning and budgeting, you can make the most of your trip and create a memorable experience without breaking the bank.

This guide will explore budgeting strategies for visitors to New Zealand, from the cost of accommodation to attractions and activities. Accommodation is likely to be one of the most significant expenses for visitors to New Zealand. The cost of accommodation varies greatly depending on the type of accommodation and location. Hotels, and guest houses are usually the most expensive options, followed by camping and holiday parks, and rental properties such as apartments and holiday homes. If you're visiting New Zealand on a tight budget, camping is the most cost-effective option. Campsites are plentiful around the country and can cost as little as $15 per night.

However, if you're after a bit more luxury, hotels and guest houses offer comfortable and affordable accommodation. Prices for a double room range from $50 to $200 per night, depending on the location and amenities.

Transportation Transportation is another major expense for visitors to New Zealand. There are a range of options available, from buses and trains to hire cars and campervans. The most economical option is to use public transport. Bus services are frequent and inexpensive, and the InterCity bus network covers most of the country. Train fares are also relatively affordable and offer a great way to explore the countryside. For those who prefer to explore New Zealand at their own pace, car hire or campervan hire is a great option. Prices start at around $50 per day for a small car and can reach up to $200 per day for a luxury vehicle. Campervan hire is also an option, with prices starting at around $100 per day for a basic vehicle. Food and Drink Food and drink is another major expense for visitors to New Zealand.

Grocery stores are plentiful and offer a range of fresh produce, as well as locally grown and produced foods. Prices vary depending on the type and quality of the product, but overall, food is relatively affordable. Restaurants and cafes are also plentiful, with prices ranging from $10 to

$30 for a main meal. Alcohol can be expensive, however, with prices for a bottle of wine or spirits ranging from $15 to $30. There is also a range of craft beers and ciders available from local breweries, which are usually a bit more affordable. Activities New Zealand is a country of incredible natural beauty, with plenty of activities to explore. Many of these activities are free or heavily discounted for students and seniors.

For those looking for a more active holiday, there are plenty of adventure activities such as hiking, kayaking, and mountain biking. Prices vary depending on the activity and location, but generally range from $20 to $50 per person. For those looking for a more relaxed holiday, there are plenty of cultural activities to explore, such as galleries, museums, and cultural performances. Prices for these activities range from free to around $30 per person. Conclusion Budgeting for a trip to New Zealand is essential for visitors who want to make the most of their visit without breaking the bank. Accommodation, transportation, food and drink, and activities are all major expenses that need to be taken into consideration. With careful planning and budgeting, visitors to New Zealand can enjoy a memorable experience without overspending.

When to visit

It is no surprise that New Zealand has become one of the top tourist destinations in the world. With so much to see and do, it can be difficult to decide when the best time to visit New Zealand is. In this part of the guide, we will explore the different factors that should be taken into consideration when deciding when to visit New Zealand, such as the climate, the prices of flights and accommodation, and the availability of attractions and activities.

The climate in New Zealand is generally mild, with temperatures rarely dropping below freezing. The summer months, from December to February, are the warmest and sunniest, with temperatures reaching an average of 23°C (73°F). During this time, the days are longer and there is less rain, making it the perfect time to explore the great outdoors. However, the summer months are also the most popular time to visit, so it can be difficult to find accommodation and flights may be more expensive. The autumn months, from March to May, offer a more temperate climate, with temperatures averaging 19°C (66°F). This is a great time to visit if you want to explore the countryside and take in the fall foliage without the crowds or high prices. It is also a great time for cycling and tramping, as the temperatures are comfortable and the rainfall is low.

The winter months, from June to August, can be colder and wetter, with temperatures ranging from 10°C (50°F) to 15°C (59°F). This is a great time of year to visit if you want to go skiing, as the ski season usually starts in late June and ends in late October. However, many attractions and activities may be closed during this time and prices may be higher. The spring months, from

September to November, are a great time to visit as the days are becoming longer and warmer. Temperatures range from 14°C (57°F) to 21°C (69°F), making it a great time for outdoor activities such as hiking and exploring. Prices may also be lower than during the summer months, so this is a great time to visit if you want to save some money.

In addition to the climate, the prices of flights and accommodation should also be taken into consideration when deciding when to visit New Zealand. Prices may be lower during the off-season months, such as winter, but flights and accommodation may be more difficult to come by. Prices may also be higher during the peak season, such as summer, but there may be more availability. It is crucial to do some research and compare prices before booking a trip. Finally, when deciding when to visit New Zealand, it is important to take into account the availability of attractions and activities. Certain attractions and activities may only be available during certain seasons, such as skiing during the winter or whale watching during the summer. It is important to plan ahead and ensure that your trip coincides with the availability of the attractions and activities that you are most interested in.

When deciding when to visit New Zealand, a variety of factors should be taken into consideration, such as the climate, the prices of flights and accommodation, and the availability of attractions and activities. By taking these factors into account, you can ensure that you have the best time possible when visiting this beautiful country.

How to get to New Zealand

New Zealand is an incredibly diverse and beautiful country, famed for its stunning landscapes, vibrant cities, and wide range of activities and attractions. Getting to New Zealand can be a daunting prospect, as it is located in the Southern Hemisphere and is quite a distance away from many parts of the world.

However, with a bit of knowledge and planning, making the journey to New Zealand is relatively straightforward. This guide will provide an overview of the different options available for getting to New Zealand, including air travel, sea travel, and road travel. Air travel is the most popular and convenient way to get to New Zealand. There are numerous international airports located throughout the country, with the two largest being Auckland and Christchurch. Direct flights are available from many major cities around the world, such as London, Los Angeles, Tokyo, and Singapore. A number of major airlines also offer connecting flights from various locations, allowing for a more cost-effective option. Depending on the specific route and airline, the flight to New Zealand can take anywhere from 12 to 20 hours. Sea travel is also an option for getting to New Zealand.

There are several cruise lines that offer trips to the country, with the most popular being P&O Cruises, Royal Caribbean, and Carnival Cruises. These cruises typically depart from ports in Australia and take between 7 and 14 days to reach New Zealand. Cruises offer a more leisurely and luxurious way of getting to New Zealand, and are usually a more cost-effective option than air travel. Road travel is not an option for getting to New Zealand, as there are no roads or bridges connecting the country to any other landmass. However, it is possible to drive to the country from Australia. There are a number of ferry services that make the journey between the two countries, the most popular being the Spirit of Tasmania.

The journey takes approximately 10 hours and can be done in either direction. In conclusion, while getting to New Zealand can seem daunting due to its location in the Southern Hemisphere, there are a number of viable options available. Air travel is the quickest and most convenient way to get to the country, while sea travel is a more leisurely and cost-effective option. Road travel is not an option, but it is possible to make the journey by ferry from Australia. With the right knowledge and planning, making the journey to New Zealand is relatively straightforward.

Traveling Documents

Traveling to New Zealand can be a thrilling and rewarding experience. Whether you're visiting for business, pleasure, or to explore the country's natural beauty, it's important to understand the necessary documents and permits you'll need in order to enter and stay within the country.

This guide will provide an overview of the different types of documents you'll need to bring with you when traveling to New Zealand, as well as the necessary application procedures. The most important document you'll need when entering New Zealand is a valid passport that has been issued by your home country. You must make sure that your passport is valid for at least three months after your intended date of departure from New Zealand. If you plan to stay longer than three months, you must also have a valid visa. Depending on your country of origin, you may be eligible for an Electronic Travel Authority (ETA) or a Visitor Visa. If you're from a country other than Australia, you'll need to apply for a Visitor Visa. If you're from an EU member state, you may be eligible for a Working Holiday Scheme visa, which allows those aged 18-30 to travel to and work in New Zealand for up to 12 months. This visa is available for a variety of countries, including the UK, France, Germany, and the Netherlands.

You can find more information about the Working Holiday Scheme visa and the countries it's available to on the New Zealand Immigration website. Once you've obtained the necessary documents and obtained your visa, you should make sure that you have the following documents with you when you enter New Zealand: -Your passport -Your valid visa -Any other documents related to your visa, such as a letter of invitation or a Certificate of Eligibility - Your return ticket or onward journey ticket - Proof of sufficient funds to support yourself during your stay -Proof of accommodation in New Zealand, such as a hotel booking confirmation If you plan to work while in New Zealand, you'll need to obtain a work permit.

This permit is usually obtained from your employer and is valid for the duration of your employment contract. It's also important to remember that you may be asked to provide proof of your identity to immigration agents upon entering New Zealand. This could include a driver's license, passport photograph, or other official documentation. If you're traveling with a group, you should make sure that each member of the group has the necessary documents to enter New Zealand. When traveling to New Zealand, it's important to be aware of the country's customs regulations. Certain items, such as firearms, drugs, and pornography, are strictly prohibited and may result in fines or arrest. It's also important to remember that New Zealand has strict quarantine laws and that any food or plant products you bring with you must be declared to customs. Finally, it's important to remember that you may be required to provide proof of health insurance upon entering New Zealand.

This requirement is in place to ensure that you are able to receive medical care in case of illness or injury during your stay. In summary, traveling to New Zealand requires a valid passport, a valid visa, and the necessary documents outlined above. It's also important to be aware of the country's customs regulations and to have proof of health insurance. By following these guidelines, you'll be able to enjoy a safe and successful visit to New Zealand.

Local Costumes and Etiquettes of the people

New Zealand is a country known for its diverse population and rich cultural heritage. From the indigenous Maori people to those of European descent, New Zealanders have a variety of local costumes and etiquettes that inform their daily lives. In this part of the guide, we will explore the local costumes and etiquettes of the people of New Zealand, looking at the traditional customs of the Maori people, as well as the more contemporary styles of dress found among the European population.

The indigenous Maori people of New Zealand have a long and rich history in the country, and their local costumes and etiquettes reflect this. Maori men often wear traditional flax cloaks or korowai, which are decorated with intricate patterns and colors. These cloaks are typically worn for special occasions or ceremonies, such as weddings or funerals. Maori women typically wear a piupiu, a skirt made of flax fibers which is often decorated with feathers and shells. In addition, both men and women wear pendants known as hei tiki, which are believed to bring good luck. In addition to traditional Maori dress, New Zealanders of European descent also have their own local costumes and etiquettes.

Europeans typically wear clothing more in line with contemporary styles found in the Western world, such as jeans, t-shirts, and sweaters. However, there are still certain cultural norms that guide how people dress in New Zealand. For instance, while it is acceptable to wear shorts and sandals in public, it is considered rude to wear tank tops or swimwear in public places. When it comes to etiquettes, New Zealanders of all backgrounds share certain common customs. For example, it is polite to address people by their first name, even those you may not know well. Additionally, it is polite to stand up when greeting someone, and it is customary to shake hands when greeting someone for the first time. It is also polite to offer to share one's food or drinks when at a dinner party or social gathering. In New Zealand, there are also certain local customs and etiquette that are unique to the Maori culture.

For example, it is important to practice the Manaakitanga, which is a form of hospitality that involves welcoming guests into one's home with respect and generosity. Additionally, it is also important to practice the Haka, a traditional Maori dance that is used to honor guests and show respect. Overall, New Zealanders have a diverse range of local costumes and etiquettes that inform their daily lives. From the traditional garments of the Maori people to the more contemporary styles of dress found among the European population, New Zealanders embrace a range of cultural customs and etiquettes that make them unique and distinct. Whether you are visiting New Zealand or living there, understanding the local costumes and etiquettes of the people of New Zealand is an important part of being respectful and aware of the local culture and customs.

Languages spoken in new Zealand

New Zealand is a culturally diverse country with a rich linguistic heritage. The country is home to over twenty different languages, with English being the primary language spoken. Māori is the most widely spoken indigenous language in the country and is considered an official language, alongside New Zealand Sign Language (NZSL) and English.

This guide will explore the various languages spoken in New Zealand, considering the history and current status of each language. English is the most commonly spoken language in New Zealand and is used in most everyday contexts. It is primarily spoken by the majority of the population, although some minority groups also use English as their native language. English is the language used in all official documents and is the language of instruction in schools. The

English language has been heavily influenced by the Māori language, which has resulted in the development of a unique dialect known as New Zealand English. Māori is the most widely spoken indigenous language of New Zealand and is an official language of the country. It is an Eastern Polynesian language and has been spoken in New Zealand for over 800 years. Māori is used in all levels of education, as well as in government and media.

The Māori language is also an important part of New Zealand culture, with many Māori words and phrases integrated into the English language. New Zealand Sign Language (NZSL) is the language of the deaf community in New Zealand and is also an official language of the country. It is a gestural language, which uses the hands, body, and facial expressions to communicate. NZSL is used in all levels of education, as well as in government and media. Other languages spoken in New Zealand include Samoan, Hindi, Cantonese, Mandarin, French, and German. These languages are spoken by various minority groups in New Zealand and are used in various contexts, such as at home and in the workplace. The status of language in New Zealand has been an important topic of discussion in recent years. The New Zealand government has implemented various initiatives to ensure the preservation of Māori language, culture, and identity.

These initiatives include education programmes in Māori, the introduction of Māori language into the school curriculum, and the establishment of the Māori Language Commission. In conclusion, New Zealand is a culturally diverse country with a variety of languages spoken within its borders. English is the most widely spoken language in

New Zealand, followed by Māori, NZSL, and other minority languages. The New Zealand government has implemented various initiatives to ensure the preservation of Māori language, culture, and identity. In this way, New Zealand is ensuring that all its citizens can access and enjoy the rich linguistic heritage of the country.

CHAPTER 3

TRANSPORTATIONS

Major Cities in new Zealand

New Zealand is a small country located in the South Pacific Ocean. It is home to some of the most beautiful landscapes and vibrant cities. From the bustling capital city of Wellington to the picturesque city of Queenstown, New Zealand is dotted with major cities that are unique in their own right.

This guide will explore the major cities in New Zealand and discuss their characteristics, attractions, and importance to the country. The capital city of New Zealand, Wellington, is located at the southern tip of the North Island. It is the third-most populous city in the country and is known for its vibrant culture, stunning harbour, and breathtaking views. Wellington is a hub for government, business, and the arts. It is home to the New Zealand Parliament, the National War Memorial, and the Museum of New Zealand Te Papa Tongarewa. It is also a popular destination for tourists, who come to explore the city's many attractions, such as the Wellington Cable Car, the Wellington Zoo, and the Wellington Botanic Garden. Auckland, New Zealand's largest city, is located on the North Island. It is a multicultural city, and its population is made up of people from all over the world.

It is a vibrant city that is home to some of the country's most iconic attractions, such as the Sky Tower, the Auckland Art Gallery, and the Auckland Zoo. The city is also home to some of the country's best shopping, dining, and entertainment venues, making it a popular destination for visitors.

Christchurch, New Zealand's second-largest city, is located on the east coast of the South Island. The city is known for its stunning natural scenery and is home to some of the country's most iconic landmarks, such as the Christchurch Cathedral and the Canterbury Museum.

The city is also a popular destination for visitors, who come to explore its many attractions, such as the International Antarctic Centre and the Christchurch Botanic Gardens. Queenstown is a small city located in the South Island. It is known for its spectacular landscapes and is a popular destination for adventure-seekers, who come to take part in activities such as skiing, snowboarding, and bungee jumping. The city is also home to some of the country's best restaurants, galleries, and boutiques, making it a popular destination for visitors. Hamilton is the fourth-largest city in New Zealand and is located on the North Island. It is known for its diverse culture and is home to some of the country's most iconic landmarks, such as the Hamilton Gardens and the Waikato Museum. The city is also a popular destination for visitors, who come to explore its many attractions, such as the Hamilton Zoo and the Hamilton Botanic Gardens.

Tauranga is a port city located on the Bay of Plenty in the North Island. It is known for its stunning beaches and is home to some of the country's most iconic attractions, such as the Tauranga Art Gallery and the Tauranga Museum.

The city is also a popular destination for visitors, who come to explore its many attractions, such as the Tauranga Harbour and the Tauranga Botanic Gardens.

Dunedin is a university city located on the south coast of the South Island. It is known for its vibrant culture and is home to some of the country's most iconic attractions, such as the Otago Museum and the Dunedin Public Art Gallery. The city is also a popular destination for visitors, who come to explore its many attractions, such as the Dunedin Botanic Garden and the Otago Peninsula. These major cities in New Zealand are some of the most vibrant and interesting places in the country. They each have their own unique attractions and culture, making them a great destination for visitors from all over the world. Each of these cities is important to the country in its own way, providing a wide range of opportunities for both locals and tourists. From the stunning harbour views of Wellington to the adventure-filled attractions of Queenstown, New Zealand's major cities offer something for everyone.

CONVEYANCE

Airports

Airports in New Zealand are an integral part of the country's infrastructure, providing vital connections to both domestic and international destinations. The aviation industry in New Zealand has seen significant growth over the past decade, with air travel now accounting for more than one-third of all passenger trips.

As such, the importance of airports in New Zealand cannot be overstated, and a closer examination of the various aspects of these facilities is necessary to understand the key role they play in the nation's transportation system. The first point to consider is the sheer scale of airports in New Zealand. The country boasts a total of six major international airports, which collectively comprise the largest airport system in the South Pacific. These airports include

Auckland International Airport, Christchurch International Airport, Wellington International Airport, Queenstown International Airport, Dunedin International Airport and Hamilton International Airport. Together, these airports serve over 30 million passengers annually, providing vital connections to the rest of the world.

The airports in New Zealand have also seen considerable investment in recent years. The government has taken steps to ensure that each airport is modern and efficient, with state-of-the-art terminals and facilities. In particular, Auckland International Airport has seen significant upgrades in recent years, with the completion of a new terminal in 2016. This terminal has been designed to offer the highest level of comfort and convenience, with world-class services and amenities. Furthermore, airports in New Zealand are well-equipped to handle a wide range of aircraft. This includes both commercial airliners and military aircraft, with the latter playing an important role in the nation's defense. Airports in New Zealand are also home to a variety of commercial and private operations, ranging from private charter operators to helicopter services. Safety is also an important factor when it comes to airports in New Zealand.

The country has a stringent set of safety regulations in place, ensuring that all airports adhere to the highest safety standards. This includes regular inspections and checks, as well as the implementation of state-of-the-art security systems. Additionally, airports in New Zealand are regularly evaluated by the International Civil Aviation Organization (ICAO), which ensures that they meet the highest global safety standards.

Finally, airports in New Zealand are also designed to be environmentally friendly. The country is committed to reducing its carbon footprint, and airports are no exception. As such, airports in New Zealand are designed with a focus on energy efficiency and sustainability. This includes the use of renewable energy sources, energy-efficient lighting, and sustainable building materials.

It is clear that airports in New Zealand play an important role in the nation's transportation system. They are well-equipped and provide vital connections to the rest of the world. Additionally, airports in New Zealand are subject to stringent safety regulations and are designed to be environmentally friendly. As such, airports in New Zealand are an integral part of the country's infrastructure, and they will continue to play an important role in the nation's future.

Taxi

Taxi services have become an integral part of the transportation landscape in New Zealand. Since the first taxi was introduced to Auckland in 1884, the industry has grown to become a vital component of the country's transportation infrastructure. This write-up provides an in-depth analysis of the taxi industry in New Zealand, including an overview of the industry's history, its current structure, the challenges it faces, and potential solutions to those challenges.

The history of the taxi industry in New Zealand dates back to the late 19th century. The first taxis were introduced in Auckland in 1884, and the industry quickly spread to other cities and towns. Over the years, the industry has underwent various changes. For instance, in the early 1900s, petrol-powered taxis were introduced, followed by the first motorized taxis in the 1930s. In the 1950s, the industry began to be regulated by the government and a number of taxi associations were established. The taxi industry in New Zealand is now highly regulated and is governed by the Transport Services Licensing Act 1989. The act requires taxi operators to obtain a license from the New Zealand Transport Agency (NZTA).

The license is valid for a period of three years and can be renewed upon application. Licensing fees vary depending on the size and type of vehicle. Taxi operators are also required to comply with safety requirements such as installing security cameras and providing a fare estimate before the ride. The taxi industry in New Zealand has faced a number of challenges in recent years. One of the key challenges is the emergence of ride-sharing services such as Uber and Lyft. These services have significantly disrupted the traditional taxi industry and have caused a decline in the number of taxi trips. Another challenge is the increasing costs of operating a taxi, such as rising fuel prices and rising insurance premiums.

Finally, there has also been a decline in the number of taxi drivers due to an aging population and a lack of younger drivers entering the industry. In order to address these challenges, the government has taken a number of steps. For instance, it has introduced a range of incentives to encourage taxi drivers to remain in the industry.

This includes providing tax credits for taxi drivers and providing access to low-interest loans. In addition, the government has also introduced regulations to protect existing taxi operators, such as reducing the number of ride-sharing vehicles on the road. Additionally, the government has also introduced measures to encourage the adoption of new technologies, such as mobile payment systems and GPS-based vehicle tracking systems. Overall, the taxi industry in New Zealand is facing a number of challenges, but the government is taking steps to address these issues. With the right incentives and regulations in place, the industry can continue to thrive and provide an essential transportation service for New Zealanders.

Car Rentals

Car rental in New Zealand is a popular option for tourists and locals alike. With its unique and varied landscape, New Zealand is a great place to explore by car. Whether you plan to explore the North Island or South Island, there are plenty of car rental providers to choose from. This guide will provide an overview of car rental in New Zealand and provide tips on how to get the best deal.

The first step in renting a car in New Zealand is to decide what type of car you need. There are many different types of vehicles available, including small cars, SUVs, minivans, and luxury cars. Depending on the size of your group or the type of terrain you plan to explore, you may need to choose a different type of car. You should also consider the availability of car rental companies in your destination, as some areas may have limited choices. Once you have chosen the type of car you need, you can begin comparing prices. Most car rental companies in New Zealand offer a variety of rental plans, including daily, weekly, and monthly rates. You can also find discounts for early booking and special offers for long-term rentals. Additionally, you should look for any additional fees, such as insurance, that are associated with the rental.

When you are ready to book a car rental in New Zealand, it is important to read the terms and conditions of the rental agreement. You should also look for any additional fees that may apply, such as airport transfer or additional charges for young drivers. Additionally, you should make sure you understand any restrictions on the rental, such as mileage limits or age restrictions. Finally, if you plan to use a car rental service in New Zealand, you should always check the reputation of the company. Many car rental companies are affiliated with international organizations and have an established reputation for providing quality service. You can find reviews of car rental companies online or ask your friends and family for recommendations.

By following these tips, you can ensure that you get the best car rental deal in New Zealand. Whether you are looking for a small car for a day trip or a luxury car for an extended holiday, you can find the perfect car rental in New Zealand. With a little bit of research and planning, you can have a great time exploring New Zealand by car.

Train Stations

Train stations are an integral part of the New Zealand transportation system, connecting communities and allowing for the easy and efficient exchange of goods and services. We will explore the history and evolution of train stations in New Zealand, their current uses and purpose, and their future potential.

The first train station in New Zealand was opened in 1867 in Otahuhu, Auckland. It was a simple structure, consisting of just one platform and a ticket office. The station was designed to transport goods from Auckland to Onehunga. Over the years, the importance of the railway network in New Zealand increased, with more stations being built and the railway network expanding to other regions of the country. In the present day, train stations in New Zealand are used to transport both cargo and passengers.

They are an important part of the nation's public transportation network, providing an efficient and cost-effective way to travel between cities and towns. The stations are well-equipped with modern amenities such as ticket machines, ticket counters, and waiting rooms.

Additionally, many stations have added features such as cafes, retail stores, and other services to make the experience more enjoyable for travelers. The future of train stations in New Zealand is promising. With the focus on sustainability and green initiatives, train stations are becoming more efficient and environmentally friendly. Several stations have been retrofitted with solar panels and wind turbines to generate electricity and reduce their carbon footprint. Furthermore, the introduction of electric trains has made it possible to reduce energy consumption and emissions. In addition to the environmental benefits, train stations in New Zealand are also being designed to be more accessible for all passengers. Many stations are now incorporating features such as wheelchair and ramp access, as well as tactile indicators for visually impaired travelers.

This has made it easier for passengers with disabilities to access the station and travel in comfort. Finally, there are also plans to make train stations more interactive and engaging for passengers. For example, there are plans to introduce virtual reality and augmented reality experiences which will make the waiting experience more interesting. Additionally, stations may also incorporate interactive displays, interactive maps, and other features which will make the experience more immersive and enjoyable. Overall, train stations in New Zealand are an important part of the nation's public transportation network. They have seen significant improvements over the years and continue to evolve to meet the needs of passengers. With the focus on sustainability, accessibility, and interactive experiences, the future of New Zealand's train stations looks bright.

CHAPTER 4

ACCOMMODATIONS

Hotels

Hotels in New Zealand are an increasingly popular destination for tourists, business travellers, and locals alike. With its stunning landscapes, vibrant cities, and many activities and attractions, New Zealand has something to offer everyone. But with such a wide range of options, it can be difficult to know which hotel is the best fit for your needs.

This guide provides a thorough overview of the hotel industry in New Zealand. It explores the various types of accommodation available, the key considerations for choosing a hotel, and the advantages and disadvantages of each type. To begin, it is important to understand the various types of accommodation available in New Zealand. Hotels are the most common type of accommodation, and range from budget to luxury options. Bed and breakfasts offer a more intimate, homely experience, while hostels provide a cheaper, more communal option. Serviced apartments are a great choice for longer stays, and holiday parks provide a range of affordable accommodation options.

When choosing the right hotel for your needs, there are a few key considerations to keep in mind. Price is one of the most important factors, but it is important to consider the location, amenities, and reputation of the hotel. It is also important to check online reviews to get a better understanding of how other guests have experienced the hotel. Other considerations include the size of the hotel, the types of services and facilities offered, and the quality of the staff. There are a number of advantages to staying in a hotel in New Zealand. Hotels offer a wide variety of amenities, such as on-site restaurants, bars, swimming pools, and fitness centres. Many hotels also provide services such as room service, laundry, and concierge services. Hotels provide a safe, secure environment for guests, and are often located close to tourist attractions and other points of interest.

On the other hand, there are also some potential drawbacks to staying in a hotel. Hotels can be expensive, and often require guests to pay for additional services, such as parking and internet access. Hotels can also be crowded, noisy, and impersonal. In addition, hotels often have strict check-in and check-out times, and may not be suitable for people with allergies or pets. In conclusion, hotels in New Zealand provide a wide range of accommodation options for visitors. When choosing a hotel, it is important to consider the price, location, amenities, and reputation of the hotel. It is also important to be aware of the advantages and disadvantages of each type of accommodation. By taking the time to research and compare different hotels, it is possible to find the perfect hotel for your needs.

Resorts

New Zealand is known for its breathtakingly beautiful landscapes and its incredibly diverse range of resorts. From luxurious beachside villas to rustic mountain getaways, there is something for everyone in this incredible country. Whether you are looking for a romantic escape, a family holiday, or a chance to explore the natural wonders, there is a resort to suit your needs in New Zealand.

When it comes to resorts in New Zealand, there are a few things to consider before booking. Firstly, you should research the location and the facilities available. Many resorts feature a wide range of activities and amenities, including swimming pools, spa treatments, golf courses, and other recreational activities. It is also important to research the resort's safety measures, such as security and medical care if necessary. When it comes to accommodation, there are a few different types of resorts in New Zealand. Luxury resorts offer the highest level of comfort and amenities, but come with a steeper price tag. Budget resorts are often cheaper and provide basic amenities, but are often lacking in quality.

For those looking for an affordable yet comfortable stay, mid-range resorts provide a great balance between comfort and affordability. When it comes to activities, there is plenty to do in New Zealand. From skiing and snowboarding to fishing and diving, the country has something to offer for everyone. Many resorts feature their own recreational activities, such as horse riding, mountain biking, and kayaking, while others feature nearby attractions. Adventure seekers can also find activities such as bungee jumping, skydiving, and heli-skiing. Finally, it is important to consider the cultural aspects of a resort in New Zealand. Many resorts feature traditional Maori culture, as well as activities such as cultural tours and performances. For those looking for a truly unique experience, some resorts offer traditional Maori ceremonies and rituals that visitors can partake in. Overall, New Zealand has a wide range of resorts to choose from.

Whether you are looking for a luxurious escape, a budget getaway, or an adventure-filled holiday, there is a resort in New Zealand for you. Be sure to research the resort's location and amenities, as well as the safety measures taken, to ensure you have the best experience possible. With so many options available, you are sure to find the perfect resort for your next vacation in New Zealand.

Camping Sites

New Zealand is home to some of the most breathtaking camping sites in the world. From the majestic mountain peaks of the Southern Alps to the stunning coastlines of Auckland and Northland, the country offers a wide range of camping opportunities. Whether you're looking for a peaceful getaway in the countryside or an adventurous weekend away in the wilderness, there is something for everyone.

To help you choose the perfect camping site for your next holiday, this guide will provide an overview of the different types of camping sites in New Zealand and the amenities they offer. The most popular type of camping site in New Zealand are the DOC (Department of Conservation) Campsites. These sites are managed by the Department of Conservation and offer a range of amenities, such as toilets, showers, and potable water. The DOC also maintains a network of tracks, huts, and campsites throughout the country, providing access to some of the most stunning natural scenery in the world. D

OC campsites are usually located near popular tourist attractions, such as Mount Cook or Queenstown, and often offer a range of activities, such as fishing, tramping, hunting, and mountain biking. Another type of camping site in New Zealand is the privately-run campsite. These sites are usually located near popular tourist attractions and offer a range of amenities, such as toilets, showers, and potable water.

Private campsites often have an associated fee, but the amenities they offer can often be superior to those of the DOC campsites. Private campsites are also often located near popular tourist attractions, such as Milford Sound or the Franz Josef Glacier. For those who are looking for a truly unique camping experience, there are also the freedom camping sites in New Zealand. These sites are usually located in remote, rural locations and are free of charge. However, these sites usually have no facilities and it is important to bring your own camping gear and supplies. Freedom camping sites also often require visitors to practice a Leave No Trace camping ethic, meaning that all rubbish and human waste must be disposed of responsibly.

No matter which type of camping site you choose, New Zealand offers a wide range of camping opportunities for all kinds of travelers. From the DOC campsites with their abundance of amenities to the freedom camping sites with their unique backcountry experience, there is something for everyone. With a bit of research and planning, you can find the perfect camping site for your ncxt holiday in New Zealand.

Here are some camping site that you can find in New Zealand:

1. Abel Tasman National Park DOC Campsite

2. Coromandel Forest Park DOC Campsite

3. Paparoa National Park DOC Campsite

4. Tongariro National Park DOC Campsite

5. Whanganui National Park DOC Campsite

6. Ruakuri Bush Campsite

7. Glentanner Park Centre Campsite 8. Lake Ohau Lodge Campsite

9. Kauri Cliffs Campsite

10. Kerosene Creek Campsite

11. Okarito Campsite

12. Pukenui Campsite

13. Waitomo Caves Campsite

14. Lake Tekapo Campsite

15. Fox Glacier Campsite

16. Rakiura National Park Campsite

17. Rainbow Springs Campsite

18. Whangarei Heads Campsite

19. Castlepoint Campsite

20. Karioitahi Beach Campsite

1. Abel Tasman National Park DOC Campsite: Located in the north-west corner of the South Island, the Abel Tasman National Park DOC Campsite is a great option for those looking for an idyllic beachside camping experience. The site is situated between Marahau and Totaranui and offers a range of amenities, such as toilets, showers, and potable water. There is also a range of activities to enjoy, such as kayaking, swimming, and fishing.

2. Coromandel Forest Park DOC Campsite: This campsite is situated in the Coromandel Peninsula, on the east coast of the North Island. It offers a range of amenities, such as toilets, showers, and potable water. The area is also home to a wealth of activities, such as tramping, mountain biking, and fishing.

3. Paparoa National Park DOC Campsite: This popular campsite is situated on the west coast of the South Island. It offers a range of amenities, such as toilets, showers, and potable water. The area is also home to a wealth of activities, such as tramping, mountain biking, and fishing.

4. Tongariro National Park DOC Campsite: Situated in the central North Island, the Tongariro National Park DOC Campsite is a great option for those looking for an idyllic camping experience. The campsite offers a range of amenities, such as toilets, showers, and potable

water. There is also a range of activities to enjoy, such as tramping, mountain biking, and fishing.

5. Whanganui National Park DOC Campsite: Situated on the west coast of the North Island, the Whanganui National Park DOC Campsite is a great option for those looking for an idyllic camping experience. The campsite offers a range of amenities, such as toilets, showers, and potable water. There is also a range of activities to enjoy, such as tramping, mountain biking, and fishing.

6. Ruakuri Bush Campsite: This campsite is situated in the Waikato region of the North Island, close to the town of Raglan. It offers a range of amenities, such as toilets, showers, and potable water. The area is also home to a wealth of activities, such as tramping, mountain biking, and fishing.

7. Glentanner Park Centre Campsite: This popular campsite is situated in the heart of the Southern Alps, on the south-west coast of the South Island. It offers a range of amenities, such as toilets, showers, and potable water. The area is also home to a wealth of activities, such as tramping, mountain biking, and fishing.

8. Lake Ohau Lodge Campsite: This campsite is situated in the Mackenzie Basin, on the east coast of the South Island. It offers a range of amenities, such as toilets, showers, and potable water. The area is also home to a wealth of activities, such as tramping, mountain biking, and fishing.

9. Kauri Cliffs Campsite: This popular campsite is situated on the east coast of the North Island, close to the town of Matarangi. It offers a range of amenities, such as toilets, showers, and potable water. The area is also home to a wealth

of activities, such as tramping, mountain biking, and fishing.

10. Kerosene Creek Campsite: This campsite is situated in the North Island's Bay of Plenty region, close to the town of Rotorua. It offers a range of amenities, such as toilets, showers, and potable water. The area is also home to a wealth of activities, such as tramping, mountain biking, and fishing.

11. Okarito Campsite: This campsite is situated on the west coast of the South Island, close to the town of Okarito. It offers a range of amenities, such as toilets, showers, and potable water. The area is also home to a wealth of activities, such as tramping, mountain biking, and fishing.

12. Pukenui Campsite: This popular campsite is situated in the North Island's Far North region, close to the town of Pukenui. It offers a range of

amenities, such as toilets, showers, and potable water. The area is also home to a wealth of activities, such as tramping, mountain biking, and fishing.

13. Waitomo Caves Campsite: This campsite is situated in the North Island's Waikato region, close to the town of Waitomo. It offers a range of amenities, such as toilets, showers, and potable water. The area is also home to a wealth of activities, such as tramping, mountain biking, and cave exploring.

14. Lake Tekapo Campsite: This popular campsite is situated in the Mackenzie Basin, on the east coast of the South Island. It offers a range of amenities, such as toilets, showers, and potable water. The area is also home to a wealth of activities, such as tramping, mountain biking, and fishing.

15. Fox Glacier Campsite: This campsite is situated on the south-west coast of the South Island, close to the town of Fox Glacier. It offers a range of amenities, such as toilets, showers, and potable water. The area is also home to a wealth of activities, such as tramping, mountain biking, and glacier exploring.

16. Rakiura National Park Campsite: This popular campsite is situated in the South Island's Stewart Island, close to the town of Oban. It offers a range of amenities, such as toilets, showers, and potable water. The area is also home to a wealth of activities, such as tramping, mountain biking, and kayaking.

17. Rainbow Springs Campsite: This campsite is situated in the North Island's Bay of Plenty region, close to the town of Rotorua. It offers a range of amenities, such as toilets, showers, and potable water. The area is also home to a wealth

of activities, such as tramping, mountain biking, and kayaking.

18. Whangarei Heads Campsite: This popular campsite is situated on the east coast of the North Island, close to the town of Whangarei. It offers a range of amenities, such as toilets, showers, and potable water. The area is also home to a wealth of activities, such as tramping, mountain biking, and kayaking.

19. Castlepoint Campsite: This campsite is situated on the east coast of the North Island, close to the town of Castlepoint. It offers a range of amenities, such as toilets, showers, and potable water. The area is also home to a wealth of activities, such as tramping, mountain biking, and kayaking.

20. Karioitahi Beach Campsite: This popular campsite is situated on the east coast of the North Island, close to the town of Karioitahi. It

offers a range of amenities, such as toilets, showers, and potable water. The area is also home to a wealth of activities, such as tramping, mountain biking, and kayaking.

CHAPTER 5

SIGHTSEEING

Sightseeing in New Zealand is an experience that is sure to enthrall and astound. With its spectacular natural beauty and diverse cultures, New Zealand offers a wide range of experiences that can be enjoyed by tourists and visitors alike. From lush rainforests and breathtaking mountain ranges to charming colonial towns and stunning coastlines, New Zealand offers something for everyone.

To start off any visit to New Zealand, a trip to the country's capital, Wellington, is a must. Here, visitors can experience the vibrant culture of the city, with its fascinating mix of Maori and European influences. Wellington has a variety of attractions, including the Museum of New Zealand, the National Library and the Parliament

Buildings. For those who love the outdoors, the city is surrounded by hills and bushland, offering plenty of opportunities for walking, cycling and kayaking. New Zealand is home to some of the most stunning landscapes in the world. The North Island is home to the Bay of Islands, a stunning area of coastline, with its beautiful sandy beaches and crystal clear waters. The South Island is equally spectacular, with its vast mountain ranges, picturesque lakes and glaciers.

For those looking for a more relaxing experience, the South Island is home to many tranquil bays, where visitors can soak up the sun and enjoy the peace and quiet. New Zealand is also home to a plethora of cultural attractions. The country's Maori culture is particularly prominent, and visitors can learn more about it at the Tamaki Maori Village in Rotorua. Here, visitors can take part in traditional activities such as carving, weaving and haka performances. The Te Papa Museum in Wellington is also a great place to learn more about New Zealand's history and culture. For those wanting to explore further, New Zealand is home to a number of national parks, offering an array of activities such as hiking, mountain-biking and skiing.

The Tongariro National Park is home to one of the best treks in the world, the Tongariro Alpine Crossing, while Fiordland National Park is renowned for its stunning fiords and lush rainforest. New Zealand is also place to some of the best wine regions in the world. The Marlborough region is renowned for its sauvignon blancs, while the Wairarapa region is home to some of the country's best pinot noirs. Visitors can sample some of the local wines at one of the many vineyards in the area, or take a tour of the region to learn more about the art of winemaking. New Zealand is an incredible destination to explore and discover, and a visit here is sure to be an unforgettable experience. With its stunning scenery, fascinating culture and wonderful activities, it is easy to see why New Zealand is such a popular destination for tourists and visitors alike. Whether you are looking for an adventure, a relaxing holiday or just a chance to experience a new culture, New Zealand is sure to offer something for everyone.

Sightseeing places in New Zealand

1. Auckland Sky Tower: Located in the heart of Auckland, the Sky Tower is the tallest free-standing structure in the Southern Hemisphere. Standing at 328 meters, the tower offers stunning views of the city and its surrounding areas. Visitors can take the SkyWalk around the perimeter of the tower or take the SkyJump to experience a thrilling base jump from the top.

2. Milford Sound: Located in Fiordland National Park, Milford Sound is one of the most spectacular natural wonders of New Zealand. With its towering mountains, lush rainforest and deep blue waters, the area is a paradise for nature lovers. Visitors can take a cruise around the sound, enjoy a scenic flight or take a guided walk to explore the area.

3. Bay of Islands: The Bay of Islands is a stunning area of coastline located in the North Island of New Zealand. The area is home to 144

islands and offers an abundance of activities such as sailing, fishing, kayaking and swimming. Visitors can also take a tour of the area to view the historic sites, such as the Waitangi Treaty Grounds and the Stone Store.

4. Abel Tasman National Park: Abel Tasman National Park is located in the South Island of New Zealand and is renowned for its golden sandy beaches and crystal clear waters. The area is home to a variety of wildlife and offers plenty of activities such as kayaking, fishing and swimming. Visitors can also take a guided walk to explore the area and its beautiful coastline.

5. Franz Josef Glacier: Located in the Southern Alps of the South Island, Franz Josef Glacier is one of the most accessible glaciers in the world. Visitors can take a guided tour of the area to explore the stunning ice formations and take in the breathtaking views. The area also offers

plenty of activities such as helihiking, rafting and kayaking.

6. Waitomo Caves: Located in the Waikato region of the North Island, the Waitomo Caves are a network of underground limestone caves. The area is home to thousands of glowworms which create an incredible light show in the darkness of the caves. Visitors can take a guided tour of the caves to explore the area and its unique formations.

7. Rotorua: A geothermal city located in the Bay of Plenty region, Rotorua is renowned for its thermal springs and bubbling mud pools. Visitors can take a guided tour of the area to explore the unique geothermal attractions, or experience the unique Maori culture at the Tamaki Maori Village.

8. Hobbiton Movie Set: Located in Matamata, the Hobbiton Movie Set is a replica of the village

featured in the Lord of the Rings and The Hobbit films. Visitors can explore the area and its setting, with its hobbit holes, gardens and waterfalls. The area also offers plenty of activities such as guided tours, archery and pony rides.

Ancient Monuments

New Zealand is home to a wealth of ancient monuments that are considered some of the most impressive in the world. From ancient Maori fortifications to giant statues, these historic sites offer visitors a chance to explore the country's rich cultural heritage and learn about its long and fascinating history.

In this guide, we will take a closer look at some of New Zealand's most important ancient monuments, from the grandiose to the humble. The most famous of New Zealand's ancient monuments is undoubtedly the Waitangi Treaty Grounds. Located in the Bay of Islands, the Waitangi Treaty Grounds are home to the Treaty House, the first formal agreement between the Maori and the British Crown. The grounds also feature a range of other historic sites, including a carved meeting house, a carved waka (canoe), and a replica of the flagpole that was raised to signal the signing of the treaty. Another important ancient monument in New Zealand is the Wairau Bar archaeological site. Located near Blenheim in the South Island, the Wairau Bar is the oldest known archaeological site in the country, and is thought to date back to between 1350 and 1500 AD. The site contains a range of artifacts, including stone tools and the remains of a fortified Maori village. New Zealand is also home to a number of impressive statues, many of which are considered ancient monuments.

The most famous of these is the Tainui Waka, a 12 meter long, 6 meter wide canoe located in Auckland. This sculpture is a replica of the voyaging canoe used by the Maori to sail to Aotearoa (New Zealand) in the 13th century. Other notable statues in New Zealand include the giant statue of the Maori navigator Kupe, located in Wellington, and the giant statue of the Maori god Tane on the North Island. Finally, it is worth mentioning some of the smaller, but no less important, ancient monuments in New Zealand. One such site is the Akaroa Lighthouse, located in the South Island. Constructed in 1878, the lighthouse is the oldest standing building in the country, and is now a popular tourist attraction.

Another important monument is the Ancient Pa Site in Waikato, which dates back to the 1500s and is home to a range of artifacts and structures. In conclusion, New Zealand is home to a remarkable range of ancient monuments, from grandiose statues to humble lighthouses. Each of these monuments offers visitors a chance to explore the country's rich cultural heritage and learn about its long and fascinating history. Whether you are looking to gain a greater understanding of Maori culture or simply marvel at the country's impressive monuments,

New Zealand is sure to provide a rewarding experience.

Here are the ancient monuments to find in New zealand

1. **Waitangi Treaty Grounds**: Located in the Bay of Islands, this is the most famous of New Zealand's ancient monuments. It is home to the Treaty House, the first formal agreement between the Maori and the British Crown, as well as other historic sites, including a carved meeting house, a carved waka (canoe), and a replica of the flagpole that was raised to signal the signing of the treaty.

2. **Wairau Bar archaeological site**: Located near Blenheim in the South Island, this is the oldest known archaeological site in the country, dating back to between 1350 and 1500 AD. It contains a range of artifacts, including stone tools and the remains of a fortified Maori village.

3. **Tainui Waka**: A 12 meter long, 6 meter wide canoe located in Auckland, this statue is a replica of the voyaging canoe used by the Maori to sail to Aotearoa (New Zealand) in the 13th century.

4. **Kupe Statue**: Located in Wellington, this giant statue is a tribute to the Maori navigator Kupe.

5. **Tane Statue**: Located on the North Island, this giant statue is a tribute to the Maori god Tane.

6. **Akaroa Lighthouse**: Constructed in 1878, this is the oldest standing building in New Zealand, and is now a popular tourist attraction.

7. **Ancient Pa Site**: Located in Waikato, this site dates back to the 1500s and is home to a range of artifacts and structures.

Museums

New Zealand is home to a variety of fascinating museums that offer a unique insight into the country's history, culture, and natural environment. Museums in New Zealand provide visitors with an opportunity to explore the country's rich past, learn about its vibrant present, and gain a deeper appreciation of its diverse people and cultures.

From the iconic Auckland War Memorial Museum to the quirky and eclectic Otago Settlers Museum, there is something for everyone to enjoy. Auckland War Memorial Museum is arguably New Zealand's most important and iconic museum. Located in the Auckland Domain, the museum houses a vast collection of artifacts, photographs, paintings, and documents, all of which tell the story of New Zealand's past. Visitors to the museum can explore Māori and Pacific Island culture, examine the effects of European settlement, and learn about the country's involvement in wars such as World War I and II. The museum also offers an insight into the country's natural environment, with displays on native flora and fauna, geology, and climate change.

The Otago Settlers Museum, located in Dunedin, provides a unique insight into the lives of New Zealand's earliest European settlers. The museum features a diverse collection of artifacts, photographs, and documents that tell the stories of the early pioneers and their struggles to make a life in a new country.

Visitors to the museum can explore the early days of settlement in Otago, learn about the people and cultures that shaped the region, and discover the history of the province's iconic industries. The Wairarapa Museum of Art and History, located in Masterton, features an impressive collection of art and artifacts that illustrate the history and culture of the region. The museum's collection includes works by some of the region's most talented artists, as well as artifacts from both Māori and European settlers.

Visitors to the museum can learn about the area's early European settlers and the struggles they faced, explore the effects of colonialism, and discover the stories of the region's Māori people. The museum also offers an insight into the region's natural environment, with displays on native flora and fauna, geology, and climate change.

The Te Papa Tongarewa Museum of New Zealand, located in Wellington, is the country's national museum and offers a comprehensive overview of New Zealand's history and culture. The museum's collection is vast and diverse, featuring art, artifacts, and documents from the country's Māori and European settlers, as well as from its numerous Pacific Island cultures. Visitors to the museum can explore the rich history of New Zealand's Māori people, learn about the country's involvement in wars such as World War I and II, and discover the stories of some of the country's most influential figures.

New Zealand's museums offer visitors a unique opportunity to explore the country's rich past, learn about its vibrant present, and gain a deeper appreciation of its diverse people and cultures. From the iconic Auckland War Memorial Museum to the quirky and eclectic Otago Settlers Museum, there is something for everyone to enjoy.

New Zealand's museums provide an invaluable resource for visitors looking to gain a better understanding of the country and its people. how many museume are there in new zealand There are more than 200 museums in New Zealand, with many of them located in the country's larger cities. Some of the most popular museums include the one I just menssion

Shopping

Shopping in New Zealand is an experience like no other. Not only is the country known for its breathtaking scenery and outdoor activities, but its shopping culture has something to offer for everyone. From high-end department stores to local markets, New Zealand has a wealth of shopping options to choose from. Whether you're looking for designer labels or bargains, shopping in New Zealand will not disappoint.

New Zealand's major cities such as Auckland and Wellington are home to a variety of shopping experiences. The larger cities offer the usual department stores, specialty shops, and large shopping malls that can be found in most countries.

These stores are usually home to a wide variety of fashion labels, electronic devices, and home furnishing essentials. For those looking for a more unique shopping experience, there are also plenty of boutiques, independent stores, and local markets. One of the most popular shopping experiences in New Zealand is the local market. These markets are a great place to find unique handmade items, fresh produce, and second-hand items. Many of these markets are held on weekends and will often feature a variety of entertainment and activities.

Shopping at local markets is a great way to immerse yourself in the culture of New Zealand and to find unique and affordable items. Online shopping is also becoming increasingly popular in New Zealand.

The internet has opened up a world of possibilities for shoppers, providing access to a wide variety of products. Online shopping is often more convenient than shopping in stores, as it can be done from the comfort of your own home. There are also plenty of online-only stores and discount websites offering great deals on items. Shopping in New Zealand is a great way to discover the culture, find unique items, and experience the beauty of the country.

No matter what type of shopping experience you're looking for, New Zealand has something to offer. Whether you're looking for high-end fashion, local markets, or online bargains, New Zealand has it all. list and explain the local market and modern market in new zealand that a tourist need to know Local markets in New Zealand are a great way to experience the culture and find unique and affordable items.

These markets are usually held on weekends and feature a variety of entertainment and activities. They are a great place to find handmade items, fresh produce, and second-hand items. They are also a great way to meet local people and explore the culture. Modern markets in New Zealand are typically found in larger cities and are home to a variety of fashion labels, electronic devices, and home furnishing essentials. These stores are usually found in large shopping malls and offer a more traditional shopping experience. They are a great place to find what you're looking for, and many of the larger stores offer discounts and sales. They are also a great way to get a sense of the current trends in fashion and technology in New Zealand.

CHAPTER 6

FOOD AND DRINKS

New Zealand offers a diverse array of food and drinks that can appeal to all palates. From the traditional Maori cuisine to modern fusion dishes, New Zealand has something for everyone.

The country's unique location makes it an ideal destination for food and drinks, with a temperate climate and access to both the Pacific and Indian Oceans. This guide will explore the food and drinks in New Zealand, with a particular focus on regional specialties and traditional dishes. The traditional Maori cuisine of New Zealand is an important part of the country's culture and heritage.

It is characterized by a diversity of dishes based on seafood, as well as plants, animals, and birds. Common Maori dishes include steamed mussels in a creamy sauce, chicken and pork dishes cooked in an earth oven, and seafood dishes such as pāua (abalone) and kina (sea urchin). Traditional desserts include poi (a thick pudding made from mashed potatoes and flour), and hāngi (a method of slow-cooking food in an earth oven).

In addition to traditional Maori dishes, New Zealand also has a range of modern fusion dishes. These dishes combine elements of the traditional Maori cuisine with those of other cultures, such as European, Asian, and Pacific Island cuisines.

Examples of popular fusion dishes include the Hangi Burger, which combines the traditional Maori hāngi with a beef patty, and the Pacific Island-inspired koku, a seafood-based soup. When it comes to drinks, New Zealand has something for everyone. The most popular beverages in the country include beer, cider, wine, and spirits. Craft beer has become increasingly popular in recent years, with local breweries producing a range of styles, such as pale ales, IPAs, and stouts.

Cider is also widely available in New Zealand, with a range of sweet and fruity flavors. Wine is produced in most regions of the country, with Marlborough and Hawke's Bay producing some of the best-known New Zealand wines. Spirits are popular in New Zealand, with whisky and gin being the most popular.

New Zealand also has a range of non-alcoholic drinks, such as fruit juices, soft drinks, and tea. Fruit juices are widely available and are made from a variety of fruits, such as apples, oranges, and kiwis. Soft drinks, such as cola and ginger beer, are also popular in the country. Tea is a popular beverage in New Zealand, with many people drinking it throughout the day. Finally, New Zealand is renowned for its delicious desserts. Popular desserts include pavlova, a meringue-based dessert topped with whipped cream and fresh fruit, and hokey pokey, a crunchy honeycomb candy.

Other popular desserts include the classic New Zealand cheesecake and the traditional Maori pudding, taro. In conclusion, New Zealand offers a wide range of food and drinks that can appeal to all tastes and budgets. From traditional Maori dishes to modern fusion dishes, there is something for everyone.

The country also has a range of alcoholic and non-alcoholic beverages, as well as delicious desserts. Whether you are looking for a traditional Maori feast or a modern fusion meal, New Zealand has something to suit every palate.

Local Cuisines

New Zealand is home to a diverse array of local cuisines that reflect the country's multicultural population and its unique geographical position. From the traditional Māori dishes of the indigenous people to contemporary fusion dishes, the country's local cuisines offer something for everyone.

Here, we will provide a comprehensive overview of the local cuisines of New Zealand and discuss why they are so popular. The Māori, the indigenous people of New Zealand, have a long-standing tradition of cooking and eating local ingredients.

This tradition is reflected in their unique cuisine, which is characterized by the use of fish, seafood, root vegetables, and wild herbs. The Māori also use a range of traditional cooking techniques such as steaming, boiling, and roasting. Common dishes include poaka (steamed pork with vegetables), kumara (sweet potato) and hāngi (meat, seafood, and vegetables cooked in an underground oven). Another important part of New Zealand cuisine is the influence of European settlers. From the late 19th century onwards, settlers from the United Kingdom, Ireland, and other countries brought their own culinary styles to the country.

This has resulted in a wide variety of dishes and the fusion of different cultures and traditions. Popular dishes include fish and chips, steak and kidney pie, and the classic Sunday roast. In recent years, the local cuisines of New Zealand have been transformed by the influx of immigrants from all over the world.

This has led to the emergence of a range of new dishes and flavours, such as Chinese-style noodles and curries, as well as Italian-influenced pasta dishes. The country's unique geographical position has also allowed for the influx of a range of exotic fruits and vegetables, leading to the creation of dishes such as tropical fruit salads and Mediterranean-style dishes.

New Zealand local cuisines are popular for a variety of reasons. For starters, they are incredibly diverse, allowing locals and visitors alike to experience a range of different cultures and flavours. In addition, the country's local foods are renowned for their freshness and quality, with many ingredients and dishes being sourced from local farms and markets. Finally, the local cuisines of New Zealand are incredibly affordable, making them widely accessible to people of all income levels.

All in all, the local cuisines of New Zealand are a testament to the country's diverse cultural heritage and its unique geographical position. From traditional Māori dishes to fusion dishes created by immigrants, the country offers something for everyone. Whether you're looking for an exotic flavour or a classic meal, New Zealand's local cuisines have something to offer.

Local Drinks

New Zealand is renowned for its wide range of local drinks, from classic beers to unique craft ciders. From the traditional to the contemporary, each beverage has its own distinct flavour and characteristics, with each region boasting its own unique blend of drinks. We'll will also explore some of the most popular local drinks in New Zealand, delving into the history and culture behind each beverage.

The first local drink we'll explore is beer. New Zealand's brewing industry has a long and rich history, with the first beers being brewed in the late 1800s. Beers from New Zealand are known for their strong hop character and full-bodied flavour. Popular beers from New Zealand include Lion Red, Steinlager, and Tuatara. Lion Red is a classic New Zealand lager brewed with a blend of New Zealand hops, giving it a crisp and refreshing taste. Steinlager is a light and aromatic beer with a slightly spicy finish. Last but not least, Tuatara is a craft beer brewed with a unique combination of New Zealand hops and malts, giving it a robust and complex flavour.

Next up is cider. Cider has become increasingly popular in New Zealand in recent years, with the craft cider industry growing rapidly. Ciders from New Zealand are often dry and refreshing, with most ciders being made from a blend of local apples. Popular ciders from New Zealand include Zeffer, Garage Project, and 8 Wired.

Zeffer is a classic dry cider with a subtle sweetness and a crisp finish. Garage Project is a craft cider made from a blend of local apples and pears, giving it a sweet and tart flavour. 8 Wired is a rich and complex cider made from a blend of New Zealand apples and hops, giving it a unique taste and aroma.

Finally, we'll look at wine. New Zealand has a long history of winemaking, and the country's wines are known for their unique character and distinctive flavour. Popular wines from New Zealand include Sauvignon Blanc, Pinot Noir, and Chardonnay. Sauvignon Blanc is a light and refreshing white wine with a crisp and vibrant taste. Pinot Noir is a medium-bodied red wine with a silky texture and layers of complex flavours. Chardonnay is a full-bodied white wine with a creamy texture and a hint of oak.

These are just a few of the local drinks that can be found in New Zealand. Each beverage has its own unique flavour and characteristics, and many of these drinks are available in a variety of styles and varieties. With so many options, there is sure to be a local drink for everyone. So why not take a tour of New Zealand's drinks and find the perfect beverage for your next adventure?

Street foods

Street food is a popular and beloved part of the culinary culture in New Zealand, with vendors selling a wide variety of cuisines from all around the world.

From spicy Asian fare to traditional Kiwi favorites, visitors to New Zealand can experience a diverse array of flavors and textures from street food vendors throughout the country. Whether you're looking for a quick snack on the go or a full meal, street food in New Zealand strikes the perfect balance between convenience and quality.

The history of street food in New Zealand dates back to the mid-19th century, when English settlers brought their recipes and culinary traditions to the South Pacific. Since then, street food vendors have evolved and adapted to the changing tastes and preferences of local customers, creating a unique style of street food that is uniquely Kiwi. Today, street vendors can be found throughout the country, from Auckland to Christchurch, serving up a variety of dishes.

The most popular street foods in New Zealand include fish and chips, samosas, and kebabs. Fish and chips are a classic Kiwi dish, with deep-fried fish and potatoes served in a newspaper cone. Samosas are small Indian-style pastries stuffed with savory fillings such as potatoes, peas, and spices. Kebabs are another popular street food, with marinated meats cooked and served on skewers with a variety of sauces and sides.

Street food in New Zealand is also heavily influenced by Pacific Island cuisine. Dishes such as taro chips, coconut bread, and mussel fritters are all popular choices. These dishes are usually served with a variety of condiments, such as chutneys, pickles, and relishes.

Street food vendors in New Zealand are highly regulated by the government. All vendors must have a permit, which is only issued after a thorough inspection of the premises and food preparation methods. The vendors must also adhere to basic food safety guidelines, such as using separate equipment for raw and cooked foods and ensuring that food is not left unrefrigerated for too long.

Street food is an important part of the culture in New Zealand, providing visitors with a delicious and convenient way to experience the country's unique culinary traditions. Whether you're looking for a quick snack on the go or a full meal, street food in New Zealand is an ideal choice. With its diverse range of flavors and textures, street food in New Zealand is sure to satisfy every palate.

CHAPTER 7

HEALTH AND SAFETY

Health and safety is of utmost importance for tourists and visitors to New Zealand. As one of the most beautiful and diverse countries in the world, New Zealand offers a variety of activities and attractions for the adventurous traveler.

From hiking to skiing, kayaking to mountain biking, New Zealand offers a wide range of outdoor activities that may pose risks to the health and safety of travelers. Therefore, it is essential to be aware of the potential hazards and take the necessary precautions to ensure a safe and enjoyable experience.

The New Zealand government is committed to providing a safe and secure environment for visitors to the country. In addition to the police, there are several public health and safety organizations that work to ensure travelers have a safe and pleasant experience. The New Zealand Transport Agency (NZTA) is responsible for road safety, while the Ministry of Health is charged with overseeing health and safety in the country. The Ministry of Business, Innovation and Employment is responsible for labor laws and regulations, and the Civil Aviation Authority of New Zealand (CAA) is responsible for aviation safety.

New Zealand has a strong culture of health and safety. For example, the country has a comprehensive system for workplace safety, as well as laws against drinking and driving. Additionally, the country has strict laws and regulations regarding food safety and hygiene. The country also has a wide range of health and safety related organizations, such as the Accident Compensation Corporation, which provides information and support to injured persons, and the Department of Labour, which provides advice and guidance on workplace safety.

When visiting New Zealand, it is important to be aware of the potential risks and take the necessary precautions. It is important to be aware of local laws and regulations regarding the use of drugs and alcohol, and to practice safe driving. Additionally, it is advisable to wear appropriate clothing and bring adequate supplies when participating in outdoor activities. It is also important to know the location of the nearest hospitals and other health care services.

In general, New Zealand is a safe and secure destination for travelers. However, it is important to be aware of the potential risks and take the necessary precautions to ensure a safe and enjoyable experience. By following the local laws and regulations, practicing safe driving, and being prepared for outdoor activities, visitors to New Zealand can enjoy all that the country has to offer while staying safe and healthy.

Vaccinations

New Zealand has long been a leader in the field of vaccinations, with a wide variety of immunization programs in place for both adults and children. Vaccinations are an important part of maintaining public health, and it is essential for travelers and visitors to understand the vaccination requirements and recommendations for New Zealand.

This guide will provide an in-depth overview of the vaccination requirements and recommendations for travel to New Zealand, as well as exploring the history, efficacy, safety, and importance of vaccinations.

As with many countries, New Zealand's vaccination requirements and recommendations are based on the World Health Organization (WHO) guidelines. Under New Zealand law, all visitors must have received certain vaccinations prior to entering the country. This includes the measles, mumps and rubella (MMR) vaccine, the diphtheria, tetanus, and pertussis (DTP) vaccine, and the varicella (chickenpox) vaccine. It is also recommended that travelers be up to date on their polio, hepatitis A, and influenza vaccinations as well. In addition, any traveler to New Zealand who has been in a yellow fever-infected area is required to present a certificate of vaccination.

Vaccinations have a long and storied history in New Zealand, with the first mass immunization program taking place in 1921. Since then, the country has worked diligently to create and maintain an effective vaccination program, which has helped to reduce the incidence of many preventable diseases. Vaccinations have been shown to be highly effective in preventing the spread of infectious diseases, with some vaccines providing up to 99% protection against certain diseases. Moreover, vaccinations are

NEW ZEALAND 2023 TRAVEL GUIDE

generally considered to be safe, with the risk of serious side effects being extremely low.

The importance of vaccinations cannot be understated. Vaccines help protect not only the individual who has received them, but also the people around them. By reducing the number of people who can become infected with a certain disease, vaccinations can help reduce the spread of the disease and, potentially, eliminate it altogether.

This is why it is so important for travelers and visitors to New Zealand to ensure that they are up to date on their vaccinations.

Despite the benefits that vaccinations can provide, there is still a small but vocal anti-vaccination movement present in New Zealand. These individuals, who are often referred to as 'anti-vaxxers', are opposed to the use of vaccinations for a variety of reasons. Some are concerned about the safety of vaccinations, while others are opposed to the idea of vaccinating children against diseases for which there is no immediate threat. It is important to note, however, that the vast majority of medical professionals and public health officials agree that the benefits of vaccinations far outweigh any potential risks.

Vaccinations are an important part of maintaining public health, and it is essential for travelers and visitors to New Zealand to understand the country's vaccination requirements and recommendations. Vaccinations have been proven to be effective in preventing the spread of infectious diseases, and they are generally considered to be safe. The importance of vaccinations cannot be overstated, as they help protect not only the individual who has received them, but also the people around them. While there may be a small anti-vaccination movement in New Zealand, the vast majority of medical professionals and public health officials agree that the benefits of vaccinations far outweigh any potential risks.

Dealing with Emergencies

Emergencies are inevitable and can occur anywhere, including New Zealand. As a tourist or visitor to this country, it is important to be aware of the risks and how to respond appropriately in the event of an emergency.

So we will discuss the various types of emergencies that can occur in New Zealand, the necessary preparation for dealing with these emergencies, and the most effective ways to respond.

The first step in dealing with emergencies in New Zealand is to understand the different types that can occur. Natural disasters such as earthquakes, tsunamis, floods, and volcanoes can occur, as can man-made emergencies such as industrial accidents or terrorist attacks. It is important to be aware of the potential risks and to be prepared for the worst.

For natural disasters, it is important to be aware of the warning signs and to have a plan in place. This should include having an emergency supply kit and knowing where to go in the event of an evacuation. It is also important to be aware of the local emergency services, such as the Civil Defence Emergency Management (CDEM) and the New Zealand Fire Service, and to know how to contact them.

For man-made emergencies, it is important to be aware of the potential risks and to take appropriate precautions. This could include being vigilant and ensuring you are familiar with your surroundings, avoiding large crowds and spaces where large numbers of people gather, and avoiding suspicious packages or objects. If you do come across a suspicious package or object, it is important to leave the area and contact the police immediately.

It is also important to have a plan for the event of an emergency. This should include having a designated meeting place, knowing the emergency services contact numbers, and having an emergency supply kit that includes food, water, medical supplies, and other essentials. In the event of an emergency, it is important to stay calm and follow the instructions of the emergency services.

In addition to being prepared for an emergency, it is important to be aware of the risks and to take appropriate precautions. This could include being vigilant and aware of your surroundings, avoiding large crowds and spaces where large numbers of people gather, and avoiding suspicious packages or objects. It is also important to be aware of the local emergency services, such as the Civil Defence Emergency Management (CDEM) and the New

Zealand Fire Service, and to know how to contact them.

Finally, it is important to know the most effective ways to respond in the event of an emergency. It is important to stay calm and follow the instructions of the emergency services. It is also important to have a plan for the event of an emergency, including a designated meeting place, knowing the emergency services contact numbers, and having an emergency supply kit that includes food, water, medical supplies, and other essentials.

Overall, emergencies can occur anywhere, and it is important to be aware of the risks and to be prepared for the worst. This includes being aware of the different types of emergencies that can occur in New Zealand, the necessary preparation for dealing with these emergencies, and the most effective ways to respond. By being aware and prepared, tourists and visitors to New Zealand can ensure that they are safe and that they can respond appropriately in the event of an emergency.

CONCLUSION

The Ultimate New Zealand 2023 Travel Guide is a comprehensive guide to experiencing the best of New Zealand over the course of a lifetime. From its spectacular beaches and lush forests to its bustling cities and rural villages, New Zealand has something for everyone. Whether it's the country's unrivaled natural beauty, its diverse culture, or its world-renowned cuisine, the Ultimate New Zealand 2023 Travel Guide is the ideal resource to help you plan and enjoy an unforgettable trip.

The Ultimate New Zealand 2023 Travel Guide is an invaluable resource for those looking to explore the many wonders of New Zealand. The guide offers detailed information on the country's most popular destinations, including North Island, South Island, and the cities of Auckland, Wellington, and Christchurch. It outlines the best ways to get around New Zealand and provides invaluable tips on where to stay, what to see and do, and where to find the best food and entertainment. It also features comprehensive sections on New Zealand's history, economy, and culture.

The Ultimate New Zealand 2023 Travel Guide is full of useful information to help travelers get the most out of their trip. From accommodation options to must-see attractions, the guide provides detailed overviews of each destination, along with information on the best times to visit certain areas. The guide also offers helpful advice on safety and health, as well as a list of useful contacts should you need assistance.

The Ultimate New Zealand 2023 Travel Guide is an essential resource for anyone looking to explore the many facets of New Zealand. Whether you're planning a short break or a long stay, the guide provides invaluable information to help you make the most of your time. From stunning beaches and lush forests to bustling cities and rural villages, New Zealand is home to many of the world's most incredible sights and experiences. With the Ultimate New Zealand 2023 Travel Guide, you can be sure of having the trip of a lifetime.

In conclusion, The Ultimate New Zealand 2023 Travel Guide is an indispensable resource for anyone looking to explore the many wonders of this unique and stunning country. With detailed information on the country's main destinations, helpful advice on safety and health, and a wealth of useful contacts, the guide is the perfect companion for anyone looking to explore the most of their New Zealand experience. From its majestic mountains to its pristine beaches, and from its vibrant cities to its rural villages, New Zealand has something to offer everyone.

With the Ultimate New Zealand 2023 Travel Guide, you can be sure of having the trip of a lifetime.

New Zealand is a country of breathtaking beauty and extraordinary experiences. From its stunning landscapes and vibrant culture to its world-renowned cuisine and bustling cities, New Zealand has something for everyone. With the Ultimate New Zealand 2023 Travel Guide, you can be sure of making the most of your time in this amazing country. Whether you're looking for an unforgettable adventure, a relaxing holiday, or just a chance to explore the many wonders of New Zealand, the Ultimate New Zealand 2023 Travel Guide is the perfect resource to help you plan and enjoy an unforgettable trip.

THANK YOU!

Made in United States
Orlando, FL
16 May 2023